Dd Ee Ff

Kk Ll Mm

Qq Rr Ss Tt

Xx Yy Zz

K Is for Kissing a Cool Kangaroo

a

b

c

For Mary – G.A.

For Pam and John Hodgson, salt of the earth – G.P-R.

Library of Congress Cataloging-in-Publication Data available

0-439-53126-8

10 9 8 7 6 5 4 3 2 1   03 04 05 06 07

Printed in Hong Kong
Reinforced binding for library use
First Scholastic edition, August 2003

K Is for Kissing a Cool Kangaroo

By Giles Andreae

Illustrated by Guy Parker-Rees

Orchard Books

An Imprint of Scholastic Inc.

New York

a is for **apple** that grows on the tree

Bb

b is for **busy** and **big bumblebee**

C c

c is for **cat** that has got all the **cream**

d is for **dragonfly**, **daisy**, and **dream**

e is for **elephant**, mighty and strong

f is for **footprints**, one hundred **feet** long

Gg

g is for **giant**, whose **garden grows** wild

H h

h is for **holding** the hand of a child

i is for **igloo**, a house made of **ice**

j is for **jellybeans** - ooh, they're so nice!

Kk

k is for **kissing** a cool **kangaroo**

l is for **loving**, like Daddy **loves** you

m is for **mischievous** m**onkey** and **mat**

n is for **naughty** and "**No**, don't do that!"

o is for **octopus**, arms everywhere

P is for **peaceful** and **piglet** and **pear**

Pp

q is for "Quickly, I've cuddled the Queen!"

R r

r is for **robot** and **racing machine**

S s

s is for **snowman** and **sister** and **snake**

t is for **teatime,** so let's have some cake!

u is for **unicorn**, **uncle**, and **udder**

V is for **vampire** whose teeth make you shudder

Vv

Yy y is for yeti and yo-yo and yes

Z z

and **Z** is for **zebra** – now how did you guess?!

On every page there are lots of other things you may have missed.

See if you can find them . . . then check them on this list!

A a
armadillo

antelope

ant

bull

B b

balloon

beetle

C c
caterpillar

cake

clouds

dalmatian

dog

D d

duck

E e
emerald

emu

eagle

ferret

F f

flamingo

frog

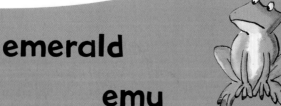

Gg

giraffe
goat
gnu

Hh

house
hamster
hyena

Ii

icicle
iguana
ibis

Jj

jester
jaguar
jam

Kk

koala
kitten
kiwi

Ll

llama
ladybug
lynx

Mm

milk
mango
mole

Nn

nectarine
newt
nest

Oo

olives
owl
otter

Pp

pelican
porcupine
pirate ship

Qq

quiche

quail

quack

raccoon

rose

Rr

rat

Ss

skunk

toucan

seal

salamander

Tt

teddy bear

turtle

Uu

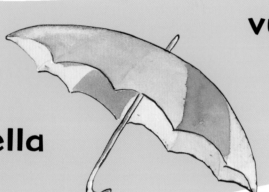

umbrella

vulture

violet

Vv

vole

Ww

weasel

woodpecker

wombat

X ray

Xx

Yy

yak

zinnia

Zz

Aa Bb Cc

Gg Hh Ii Jj

Nn Oo Pp

Uu Vv Ww